WHAT EVERY FUTURE WIDOW

SHOULD KNOW

(AND WIDOWER, TOO)

By

Harry Mautner

Certified Public Accountant

ISBN: 0-7596-8051-5

Library of Congress Control Number: 2002093077

This book is printed on acid free paper.

Printed in the United States of America

Bloomington, IN

1stBooks - rev. 07/09/02

To the true love of my life, my wife.

THIS BOOK IS NOT INTENDED TO PROVIDE ANY ACCOUNTING, LEGAL OR FINANCIAL ADVICE. CONSULT YOUR ACCOUNTANT ATTORNEY AND FINANCIAL ADVISOR FOR ADVICE REGARDING A SPECIFIC COURSE OF ACTION SUITED TO YOUR INDIVIDUAL REQUIREMENTS.

IF YOU DO NOT PLAN YOUR ESTATE, NO ONE ELSE WILL. EITHER YOU LEAVE YOUR MONEY TO YOUR FAMILY WITH PROPER PLANNING OR YOU WILL LEAVE IT TO 280 MILLION STRANGERS. OUR GOVERNMENT HAS THE SPENDING HABITS OF SOME OF OUR CHILDREN.

DO NOT POSTPONE READING THIS BOOK UNTIL THERE IS A CRISIS IN YOUR LIFE. EVERYONE, MARRIED OR SINGLE CAN BENEFIT FROM THE INFORMATION IN THIS BOOK.

FOREWORD

For better or for worse, using the language of the wedding ceremony, wives outlive husbands.

For a widow, grief is a normal reaction to the death of her husband and such feelings should not be held back.

However, bewilderment about your financial affairs does not have to follow. Concern over your money and investments is not an emotional reaction, but is an intellectual reaction which can be avoided if you are aware of and are familiar with your financial affairs.

Many people become uptight when numbers, assets or liabilities are discussed. They believe that these are complicated subjects and are difficult to understand.

The objective of this book is to take the mystery out of what you believe to be a complicated subject and to make them simple for you to understand. You can learn to manage your own financial life.

Let us take the first step together!

TABLE OF CONTENTS

TESTAMENTARY TRUST

IRREVOCABLE TRUST

CHARITABLE REMAINDER TRUST

QUALIFIED PERSONAL RESIDENCE TRUST

Q TIP TRUST

Q DOT TRUST

MARITAL TRUST

WHAT I OWN

WHAT I OWE

ACKNOWLEDGEMENT

The motivation for this book was the frustration experienced by many of my clients who survived their spouses. Many times most financial activities are handled by only one spouse without the participation of the other. I hope that the pain that I saw in some of my clients can be avoided by many individuals after reading this book.

I wish to thank my family for their encouragement in writing this book and for their helpful suggestions. Especially my sister in law, Ruth Silverstein, who I feel is my sister, for her support and suggestions.

Special thanks to my wonderful wife, Milly, who was diligent in her proof reading and her common sense suggestions regarding its content. This book, as well as any of my accomplishments, would not be possible without her.

BEFORE YOU DO ANYTHING ELSE - AVOID

PROBATE

BEFORE YOU DO ANYTHING ELSE-AVOID PROBATE

To die is bad enough. But to die leaving only a Will, or without a Will, is much worse. Your spouse or executor, or personal representative, as it is called in some states, will have the frustration and expense of dealing with an attorney and the probate court in order to carry out your wishes. A widow will feel very powerless if she needs an attorney in order to collect that which is due her according to her husbands wishes. If you or your spouse die without leaving a Will, the State will choose your heirs. You certainly do not want that to happen.

If your signature is necessary to transfer anything that you own at your death the probate process becomes necessary. If you die leaving a Will, that Will must be probated in a court. Probate is the state court procedure to distribute a decedent's assets according to his Will. All Wills require this probate procedure. If the decedent has property in another state, his estate must go through the probate process in that state as well. All probate proceedings are open to the public scrutiny. All your financial affairs become open to the public.

By contrast, if the decedent has a Revocable Living Trust there is no probate procedure required and no facts regarding your estate become public knowledge. The Trustee of the Revocable Living Trust has full power to distribute the decedent's assets without requiring the services of an attorney or seeking permission from a court.

Probate can be both time consuming and expensive. Legal fees can average between 3% and 6% of the total assets of the deceased. The probate procedure can last months or even years before the deceased's assets are distributed. As your husband's survivor you will feel frustrated in your inability to collect your husbands assets without the services of an attorney and with the time delay of court proceedings and the expense of legal fees.

You do not want to go through that hassle and expense.

There are only three ways to transfer assets owned by a deceased:

1. By a Last Will

2. By operation of law

3. By a Revocable Living Trust

Examples of such transfers:

Assets owned individually by decedent

must be probated

distributed according to Will

Assets owned as joint tenants with right of survivorship

distributed to surviving joint owner, without probate

Assets owned as tenants in common

decedent's share distributed according to Will

survivor's share continues as before

Assets held "In trust for"

distributed to named beneficiary

Assets owned by Revocable Living Trust

distributed, WITHOUT PROBATE, according to terms of the

Revocable Living Trust

LAST WILL

Every Will must be probated in a court. The court must grant permission to the named executor or personal representative to act in that capacity. You will need an attorney to accomplish this. Most attorneys will charge between 3% and 6% of the total assets of the estate. You will constantly need the services of an attorney. You will be faced with delays of months or years.

These negative by products of leaving only a Will have been repeated to emphasize the disadvantages of a Will. This is true whether one leaves a small estate or millions of dollars.

OPERATION OF LAW

Examples of transfer by operation of law are joint bank accounts and proceeds of insurance policies or annuities where a surviving beneficiary is named.

DISADVANTAGES OF JOINT ACCOUNTS

Holding assets in joint account does avoid probate but there is a price to pay for that privilege.

Those assets are subject to creditor claims of both joint tenants.

Those assets can not be used to fund a By Pass Trust for your spouse because they automatically become the property of the survivor. See page nine for the benefits of a By Pass Trust.

Those assets can be withdrawn by one joint tenant without the permission of the other joint tenant.

Those assets will partially lose it's stepped up basis. All assets of a deceased are valued, for estate tax purposes, at their market value as of the date of death. That value becomes the cost basis when the asset is sold. The cost basis of assets held in joint account is computed as one half of the fair market value at date of death and one half of the original cost, which usually results in a lower cost basis in the event of sale. The exception to this rule is when one lives in a community property state. In that case the assets are valued at their fair market value.

Those assets will eventually be again subject to estate taxes when the surviving joint tenant passes away.

A joint account with a child is not recommended because, in addition to the problems shown above, assets held in joint account with a child are subject to spousal claims in the event of a divorce. Also, where there are several children and some live in another state, there is a tendency on the part of the parent to name the child living locally as joint tenant. This results in the local child inheriting the entire amount of the joint account.

A joint account is not the best way to title your assets because of all the preceding.

REVOCABLE LIVING TRUST

One does not have to be rich in order to receive the benefits of a Revocable Living Trust.

Whatever asset is titled in the name of the Trust will avoid the probate process.

Do not be alarmed by the words Revocable Living Trust. Simply put, the Trust is a set of papers, prepared by an attorney, which describes your

7

wishes regarding the assets held by the Trust while you are alive and also after your death.

You can be the sole Trustee who manages the trust assets or you can name a Co Trustee.

You can take out all the income of the Trust as well as take out any part of the principal.

You can amend any provision of the Trust or cancel it entirely.

You can add or remove assets from the Trust.

No separate income tax return is required for the Trust. You will prepare your income tax return in the same way that you do now.

You must name a successor Trustee to succeed you in the event of your disability or death. By naming a successor Trustee you will avoid the time consuming and legally expensive proceedings where a court will name a guardian for you in the event of your inability to manage your own affairs. There is no requirement for a court to name your spouse or child as your guardian. The judge can choose anyone he pleases.

Most Revocable Living Trusts contain a By Pass Trust provision. In the typical husband and wife situation where the husband leaves his wife all of his assets there is no estate tax due. However, when the second spouse dies the entire estate of both husband and wife, now owned by the survivor, will be subject to estate taxes. Under present law, up to the end of 2003, the first $1,000,000.00 of assets are not subject to estate taxes. This exemption will increase gradually until it becomes $3,500,000.00 in the year 2009, under the estate tax law passed in 2001.

BY PASS TRUST

The By Pass Trust, sometimes called a Marital Trust a Credit Shelter Trust or an "A" "B" Trust, or a Residuary Trust, allows the assets in that Trust not to be subject to estate taxes when the surviving spouse passes away. The Trust allows the surviving spouse to receive all of the income earned by the Trust. The spouse also has the right to take a portion of the principal of the Trust for his or her maintenance, support or medical or nursing care.

It is important to create a separate Revocable Living Trust for both husband and wife in order for each to receive the lifetime estate tax exemption. If there is no objection, divide all your assets equally and transfer each half to each spouse's Trust.

In the example where a husband leaves his entire estate to his wife, the successor Trustee of the husband, usually his wife, will transfer some assets from the husband's Trust to the wife's Trust and some assets to a newly created Marital Trust, sometimes called a By Pass Trust. The wording of the deceased's Revocable Living Trust is the authority for the creation of the By Pass Trust. The amount transferred to the By Pass Trust will be computed to effect the maximum estate tax savings.

For large estates the sum of $1,000,000.00, or whatever sum is exempt from estate tax in years after 2002, is placed in the By Pass Trust at the death of the maker of the Revocable Living Trust. By so doing, that sum will not be subject to the estate tax of the surviving spouse. At present, using the sum of $1,000,000.00 the estate taxes of the surviving spouse will be reduced by as much as $500,000.00.

For smaller estates, at the death of the first spouse, the amount transferred to the Marital trust should be an amount which will not make the death of the second spouse subject to estate tax. These amounts will change whenever the tax law increases the maximum size of an estate not subject to tax.

Be aware that one can only get the estate tax savings benefit of a By Pass Trust, sometimes called a Marital Trust, or an A and B Trust, while both spouses are alive.

That is the best argument for preparing a Revocable Living Trust, which will include in it a By Pass Trust, now, while both husband and wife are alive.

It is wise to keep the original of all documents prepared in your possession in a safe place.

IT DON'T MEAN A THING IF YOU DON'T HAVE THAT SWING

The Revocable Living Trust is effective only for assets titled in the name of the Trust. You must transfer the title of assets which you wish to place in the Trust. Generally, for married couples, two Trusts are created with one half of all assets owned placed into each spouse's Trust. It is usually a simple procedure to make this transfer. Simply advise your bank or brokerage house to make the transfer. Many institutions require only the first and last page of the Trust for their records. The title of the Trust will be "John Jones Trust, John Jones Trustee".

POUR OVER WILL

In addition to the Revocable Living Trust your attorney will prepare a Last Will to provide for disposition of any asset that is not titled in the name of the Trust, such as personal effects. This is called a Pour Over Will.

OTHER DOCUMENTS

As part of your estate plan your attorney will prepare the following documents:

Revocable Living Trust

Pour Over Will (needed to distribute assets not titled in your Revocable Living Trust)

Durable Power of Attorney

> This allows another person to act on your behalf. It is automatically cancelled upon your death.

Living Will

> This declares that you do not wish to have your life
> extended artificially under certain circumstances.

Health Care Surrogate

> This allows a person you name to act on your behalf in
> matters of your health or medical care when you are unable
> to act for yourself.

THE ADVANTAGES OF THE REVOCABLE LIVING TRUST

It can be changed at any time and as often as you wish.

You have complete control over your assets while you are alive.

Your successor Trustee has the power to act on your behalf to carry
out your wishes after you pass away. He does not require the permission
of a court to perform his duties.

Your successor Trustee does not need an attorney to carry out your
wishes.

There is no time delay in carrying out your wishes.

Your spouse is spared the frustration of needing an attorney and being powerless to receive the inheritance without the permission of a court. Many husbands appoint their wife as the successor Trustee, and vice versa.

There are no legal or probate fees triggered by your death.

All assets titled in the name of the Trust avoid the probate procedure.

It avoids the probate of real estate located in any state.

The Revocable Living Trust is a private document and does not have to be filed with a court. It's contents are private and are not available for public scrutiny as contrasted to a Will.

There is no necessity of court proceedings to establish your guardianship in the event of your disability.

It is more difficult for disgruntled relatives to challenge the provisions of a Revocable Living Trust than to challenge a Will.

There are no income tax filings other than your usual individual income tax form.

SHOULD YOU LEAVE MONEY TO YOUR CHILDREN OUTRIGHT OR WITHIN THE PROVISIONS OF A TRUST?

When you leave money or property outright to your child there are three potential problems.

It is subject to claims of a spouse during divorce.

It is subject to claims of your child's creditors.

It is subject to estate taxes upon the death of your child.

As an alternative, consider leaving assets to a Trust, which will be created at your death, as provided in your Revocable Living Trust, for the benefit of your child. By doing so all those problems will be avoided. The trust will allow your child to receive the income earned by the Trust during his or her lifetime. It will also make provision for the Trustee to pay part or all of the assets in the trust to your child if required for health, education or support. At the death of your child the assets held in the trust will not be included in the taxable estate of your child, thereby reducing the estate taxes payable by your child's estate. This is good long term estate planning.

It is not unusual to name one child as Trustee for another child's Trust and vice versa. The terms of the Trust can be completely flexible to represent your wishes. You can name, for example, your grandchildren as the beneficiaries of the Trust after the death of your child.

Synopsis of "Before You Do Anything Else - Avoid Probate"

All Wills must be probated in a court. This procedure is both time consuming and expensive.

There are only three ways to transfer assets owned by a decedent:

By a Last Will

> Requires probate before assets can be transferred

By operation of law

> Applicable to assets held in joint accounts

> Applicable to life insurance or an annuity where a surviving beneficiary is named

By a Revocable Living Trust

> The best and fastest way. Probate is not necessary for any asset owned by a decedent which is titled in a Revocable Living Trust.

WHAT IS INCLUDED IN YOUR TAXABLE

ESTATE?

WHAT IS INCLUDED IN YOUR TAXABLE ESTATE?

The good news is that you will never pay your estate tax. It is a tax payable nine months after your death and is payable by your executor using assets in your estate.

Your entire assets, valued at the date of your death, are included in your taxable estate. One half of jointly held assets are also included. Life insurance policies, where you are the owner of the policy, are included in your taxable estate. Policies owned by an Irrevocable Life Insurance Trust are not included.

The total taxable assets are reduced by funeral and administrative expenses, accounting and legal fees, debts owed and mortgages payable. The federal tax rate start at 37% and goes as high as 50%. In addition to the federal tax most states charge additional state estate tax. For the year 2002 the first $1,000,000.00 is exempt from the tax. That sum, called the unified credit, will increase periodically and will become $3,500,000.00 in 2009.

The estate tax amounts to progressive confiscation. In a large estate:

husband or wife keeps 100% of the inheritance

their children keep 50%

the next generation keep 25%

the following generation keep 12 ½ %

All inherited assets, for estate and income tax purposes, are valued at the fair market value at the date of death, called the "stepped up basis". When the asset is sold, the profit is computed, for income tax purposes, on the difference between the sales price and the stepped up basis.

For the years 2002 and 2003 the first $1,000,000.00 of assets, valued at fair market value, are not subject to estate taxes. That amount is called the unified credit or lifetime exemption. That amount will increase in the following years:

2004	$1,500,000.00
2005	1,500,000.00
2006	2,000,000.00
2007	2,000,000.00

2008	2,000,000.00
2009	3,500,000.00

The estate tax is scheduled to be repealed for the year 2010. For the year 2011 the unified credit goes back to $1,000,000.00.

All of the above is based on the estate tax provisions of the estate tax act passed in 2001.

THE MOST COMMON MISTAKES OF ESTATE

PLANNING

THE MOST COMMON MISTAKES OF ESTATE

PLANNING

DURING YOUR LIFETIME

1. not giving the annual amount not subject to gift tax which is $10,000 per year per person plus direct payments of tuition or medical expense (assuming that you can afford to make such gifts)

2. not gifting assets which will increase in value

3. not having a Will and a Revocable Living Trust

4. having the misconception that a Will will avoid probate

5. having the misconception that probate is not required if your total assets are less than your lifetime exemption

6. being the owner of life insurance on your life

7. not having liquid assets in your estate to pay estate taxes

8. having no plan of continuity to maintain a family business

9. not being aware that pensions and IRA's are subject to both estate and income taxes, unless left to your spouse

10. having joint accounts with children

It is not necessary to itemize all your assets that you own in the preparation of your Will or Revocable Living Trust. The language of the documents will state specific requests that you make and mention the percentages of all other assets to be distributed to the individuals that you name.

BEFORE DEATH OCCURS

Instructions From The Grave

It cannot be done. Even Houdini wanted to communicate from the grave and was not successful. Instead, you can sit down with your spouse now to discuss the things you should do after the death of the first spouse. Now is the time - there may be no opportunity later. Become familiar with your financial investments and the location of important documents. Now is the time to organize whatever papers and documents that you can.

PLAN YOUR FUTURE FINANCIAL ACTIVITIES NOW

If you are accustomed to having your spouse make the major financial decisions, it would be wise to discuss with him (or her) your future financial decisions when the responsibility is yours. Make a list of all your assets and list the appropriate comment next to each type of asset. For example:

auto:	sell one car, keep the leased car
common stocks:	hire and investment advisor to help you
and	or
mutual funds	sell all stocks and reinvest proceeds in certificates of deposit
	or
	sell all stocks and reinvest proceeds in preferred stocks and corporate bonds
preferred stocks:	hold for the income you will receive
home:	keep in order to maintain your lifestyle
investment in real estate:	hold for the income you will receive

or

sell and reinvest proceeds in certificates

of deposit

It is important to get the benefit of your spouse's thinking while it is still available. This will provide you with a roadmap to follow.

Talk it over now. Do not leave it to chance.

WHEN DEATH OCCURS

WHEN DEATH OCCURS

A FINANCIAL CHECKLIST WHEN YOUR SPOUSE DIES

Get several certified copies of the death certificate

Gather the Will, Trust documents, marriage certificate, bank and brokerage statements, real estate leases and deeds and investments of all types

Apply for social security benefits (death benefit), veteran's and professional organization benefits

Get in touch with spouse's employer about retirement funds, deferred salary, stock options, accrued vacation pay, commissions, bonuses and corporate life insurance

Make sure that your medical and other insurance policies are in force

File life insurance claims

Transfer all joint accounts to your own account or preferably to your Revocable Living Trust

Transfer assets to a Marital Trust in accordance with the terms of your spouse's Revocable Living Trust. See the chapter "Before You Do Anything Else - Avoid Probate"

Transfer all other assets held by your spouse's Revocable Living Trust to your Revocable Living Trust. Such transfer can be made by you easily if you have been named Co-Trustee or Successor Trustee of your spouse's Trust. Any asset owned individually by your spouse must go through the probate process. See the chapter "Before You Do Anything Else - Avoid Probate."

See an attorney or accountant to prepare the federal estate tax return (Form 706) and a state estate tax. These forms must be filed and paid within nine months after death for estates in excess of $1,000,000.00 in 2002, with increased minimums up to $3,500,000.00 in the year 2009.

Generally, it is wise to make no important decisions shortly after the death of a spouse. This is not the time to make major changes. Allow yourself some time to cope with the trauma of the passing.

You must roll over to your IRA the amount in your spouse's IRA and corporate pension plan within sixty days after death in order to avoid its taxability. Everyone must begin taking a minimum distribution from an

IRA or pension plan upon reaching the age of 70 ½. Such distributions are computed by consulting an IRS table which determines the percentage of pension assets that you must withdraw based on your life expectancy or on a joint life expectancy of yourself and your spouse if your spouse is ten years younger than yourself.

Locate the last three years of personal income tax returns, Form 1040. It will be needed for the preparation of the federal estate tax return, Form 706, which is due nine months following death. If you cannot locate these returns, request copies from IRS.

Also locate any state and local tax forms previously filed.

THE ROLE OF LIFE INSURANCE AS AN

ESTATE PLANNING TOOL

THE ROLE OF LIFE INSURANCE AS AN ESTATE PLANNING TOOL

Buying life insurance does not decrease the estate tax due upon death. It does provide a sum payable upon death which can be used to pay for estate taxes or to add to the value of your estate. Second to die life insurance had become popular because it is payable only after the death of the second spouse. When a husband leaves his entire estate to his wife, the estate tax is payable on the wife's death. One spouse can be uninsurable and yet a second to die policy can be issued.

Life insurance proceeds payable to a second spouse are both income and estate tax free. However, when the surviving spouse dies those proceeds will be included in the taxable estate. To avoid having the life insurance proceeds being subject to estate taxes after both spouses have deceased, the life insurance policy should be owned by an Irrevocable Life Insurance Trust. Once created such a Trust cannot be changed. You will need an attorney to prepare such a Trust.

METHODS TO REDUCE THE ESTATE TAX

METHODS TO REDUCE THE ESTATE TAX

GIVE ANNUAL GIFTS

Reduce the size of your estate by giving annual gifts of $10,000.00 per person to as many people as you wish. A married couple can gift $20,000.00 to as many individuals as they please. In addition you may give amounts paid directly for tuition or medical expenses.

You may give gifts in excess of the $10,000.00 or $20,000.00 by husband and wife. The gift must be reported on a gift tax return and the excess will be deducted from your unified credit which is the amount not subject to estate taxes. This is a good way to reduce your taxable estate of assets which you anticipate increasing in value with time.

FORM A CHARITABLE REMAINDER TRUST

It is best to give appreciated assets to a charity. You will not owe income taxes on the profit you have realized. You will receive a current income tax deduction based on the fair market value of the assets donated.

For the rest of your life and the life of your spouse you will receive an income from the charity based on the market value of the gift and your joint life expectancy. After you both have deceased there will be no value left to your estates.

FORM A PERSONAL RESIDENCE TRUST

Your personal residence is placed into such a Trust which provides the following:

You have the right to live in the residence for a specific number of years with no payment to the Trust. You continue to pay taxes, maintenance, mortgage payments, etc.

At the end of that term the residence will be owned by the person that you designate in the Trust.

You enter into a lease with that person to continue to live in the residence and pay a rent based upon the fair market value.

Advantages:

Your personal residence is no longer part of your estate. The value of the residence given to the Trust is considered a gift. But that gift is valued at a percentage of the fair market value of the residence because the gift is conditional on your free occupancy during your lifetime. Based on your age and statistical tables that value could be 50% of the current fair market value of the property. If so, you have effectively eliminated 50% of the value of your residency from your taxable estate.

FORM A FAMILY LIMITED PARTNERSHIP and transfer some assets to it.

The usual format is for husband and wife to form the partnership with husband having a 1% general partnership and a 49% limited partnership interest. Wife will have the same interest. Each year, if you so desire, you each gift up to a $10,000.00 limited partnership interest to as many family members as you wish. Only the general partners can manage the partnership and make decisions regarding investments or operations of the partnership.

The savings in estate taxes follows. Because there are minority interests in the partnership, the Internal Revenue Service will allow your estate to reduce the fair market value of assets held by the partnership by a substantial percentage for estate tax valuation purposes. For example, assets with a fair market value of $1,000,000.00 could be valued a $500,000.00 thus saving your estate the tax on $500,000.00.

Also, by making annual gifts of limited partnership interests you have further reduced the size of your taxable estate.

There are many factors to consider before setting up a Family Limited Partnership. For one thing when you distribute the income of the partnership you must distribute a proportionate amount to the limited partners. In one respect this allows you to gift amounts in addition to the maximum of $10,000.00 per year.

BUY LIFE INSURANCE using an Irrevocable Life Insurance Trust

Many people become upset when they are approached by life insurance salesmen. Let's face it, life insurance companies are in the business to make money. But you must consider buying the insurance with the understanding that it will put extra money in the hands of your beneficiaries.

Assume the following facts:

If you and your spouse are 65 years old you can buy a second to die life policy of $700,000.00 for a one time payment of $100,000.00. If you both live long enough so that your payment of $100,000.00 would have earned $600,000.00 at the time of your death, the total that you invested in the policy would be the same as the amount that your beneficiary would collect. On the surface nothing has been gained. However if you did not buy the insurance the $700,000.00 in your estate would give your heirs $350,000.00 if your estate were in the 50% bracket.

The same results would follow of you paid annual premiums on the life insurance rather than pay in one lump sum.

Of course if the payment of the premium interferes with your lifestyle do not buy the insurance. Most individuals feel that their primary responsibility is toward themselves and their spouse.

POPULAR TYPES OF TRUSTS

POPULAR TYPES OF TRUSTS

A Trust is a legal document which your attorney will prepare for you. Title to an asset, or assets, is transferred to the Trustee. The Trustee will manage and administer the Trust in the same manner as you did when you owned the asset in your name. You can name yourself the Trustee. Or, if you choose, you may name yourself and your spouse as Co-Trustees.

A REVOCABLE LIVING TRUST

It is revocable at any time.

It is prepared while you are living.

You will manage your investments, additions and withdrawals in the same manner as before the Trust was created.

The income earned by the Trust is reported on your personal income tax return.

The Trust uses your personal social security number.

The Trust files no tax return.

You can add or remove assets from the Trust, requiring no change in the Trust.

For the advantages of such a Trust, see the Chapter "Before You Do Anything Else - Avoid Probate"

TESTAMENTARY TRUST

This Trust becomes effective at you death. An example of such a Trust is the Marital Trust, sometimes called a By Pass Trust, or a "A" "B" Trust, or a Residuary Trust, whose provisions are included in the Revocable Living Trust.

IRREVOCABLE TRUST

This Trust cannot be altered once it is executed. An example of such a Trust is the Irrevocable Life Insurance Trust which is designed to keep the proceeds of life insurance out of the taxable estate.

CHARITABLE REMAINDER TRUST

This is an agreement between you and a charity of your choice whereby you give a sum of money, or property, to the charity in exchange for a guaranteed income for your life or the life of you and your spouse, based on life expectancy. There is no remaining value to the Trust after lifetime payments cease.

This arrangement works best with the transfer of appreciated assets. For example, if you give stock which cost you $20 and is now worth $100, your gift is valued at $100. You pay no capital gains tax on the increase in value. You receive a charitable deduction based on $100 on your tax return. Generally, the dividends which you received on your stock will be less than the guaranteed life time income. With part of that excess you can purchase life insurance to compensate your beneficiaries for the loss to your estate of the assets placed in the Trust.

QUALIFIED PERSONAL RESIDENCE TRUST

In this type of Trust, title to your personal residence is transferred to the Trust. The Trust stipulates that you and your spouse may live in the home for a specific number of years. Should you pass away before the said number of years, the Trust is invalid. If you outlive the term of the Trust you must pay fair rental value to the Trust.

The value of your home is excluded from your taxable estate. The current fair market value of your home, less the value given to the use of the home for the specific number of years of your free occupancy, is considered a gift. Since the value of your home at death, which may have appreciated since the inception of the Trust, is greater than the reduced value of the gift, there is an estate tax saving.

Q TIP TRUST

Such a Trust provides that the income earned by the Trust be paid to a named person. After the death of the income beneficiary, the principal of the Trust will be paid to another person or persons. It is commonly prepared in the case of second marriages, providing income to one's second spouse, with the principal going to the children of the first marriage after the death of the second spouse.

Q DOT TRUST

Since a non citizen does not receive the same lifetime exemption as does a citizen, such a Trust is prepared to reduce the estate tax of a non resident.

MARITAL TRUST

It is sometimes called a By Pass Trust, an "A" "B" Trust, a Credit Shelter Trust or a Residuary Trust. It becomes effective at your death. It allows both you and your spouse's estate to claim the maximum life time exemption, sometimes called the Unified Credit, which is the amount of your estate which is not subject to estate taxes.

PRENUPTIAL AGREEMENT

PRENUPTIAL AGREEMENT

Most states require that your surviving spouse inherit a percentage of your total estate.

If you are considering remarriage and choose to leave most of your assets to your children and choose to leave less to your intended spouse, the only way to accomplish this goal is to enter into a pre-nuptial agreement with your intended spouse. Consult with an attorney who is experienced in the preparation of this type of agreement. Some states may require that a minimum amount be left to a surviving spouse.

SHOULD YOU REFUSE AN INHERITANCE?

SHOULD YOU REFUSE AN INHERITANCE?

If your spouse has left you his entire estate and you feel that the assets that you already own are more than sufficient to meet your financial needs, consider refusing the inheritance and allow the assets to pass directly to your children, or other named beneficiaries.

This will avoid having these assets subject to estate tax when you pass away.

Such a disclaimer must be in writing and made within nine months of your spouse's death. The disclaimer must be made before the assets have been transferred to you. You may not direct the disposition of these assets to the person who inherits them.

HOW MUCH AM I WORTH?

THE EASY WAY TO MAINTAIN YOUR MONEY

RECORDS

HOW MUCH AM I WORTH?

THE EASY WAY TO MAINTAIN YOUR MONEY

RECORDS

Let us start by eliminating the technical words "assets" and "liabilities" and substitute the simple phrases "what I own" and "what I owe". That should make it easier to understand your financial condition.

WHAT I OWN

Just as one cannot begin construction of a building without a set of plans, you should know and record on paper everything that you own or owe in order to know what you are worth.

The best way to keep track of what you own is to list each "what I own" (your assets) on a separate sheet of paper and keep these sheets in a ring binder. This arrangement will allow you to remove from the ring binder those assets which you sell or no longer own. If you prefer, you can keep these records on your computer.

Items To List on "what I own sheets" - examples

    bank certificates of deposit

    individual stocks

    individual bonds

    investments in partnerships

    investments in private corporations

    mutual funds

    money market accounts

    home

    automobile

    brokerage accounts

        keep a separate page for your money market

        have a page for each stock owned in alphabetical order in order to facilitate comparison of your records with the broker's statement showing the stocks being held in your account.

WHAT I OWE

Items To List on "what I owe sheets"

mortgage liabilities

auto loans payable

bank loans payable

credit card balances

You do not have to be a financial genius

Add up the market values of all your "what I own" sheets

Subtract the amounts of the "what I owe" sheets

The result is what you are worth.

It is a good idea to do this periodically, at least once a year, to determine if your net worth is increasing or decreasing.

Example of "What I Own" Sheets

XYZ Common Stock

	bought	sold	profit or loss
7-2-00			
bought 100 shares at $75.00	$ 7500.00		
commissions	+ 20.00		
	$ 7520.00		
9-10-00			
sold 100 shares at $ 81 ¼		$ 8,125.00	
commissions		- 20.00	
		$ 8,105.00	$ 585.00

Example of "What I Owe" Sheet

<u>Loan Payable To Ocean Bank</u>

	Amount		
	Paid	Owed	Balance
July 1		$ 10,000.00	
October 2	$ 2,000.00		$ 8,000.00

A CRASH COURSE IN INVESTING

(The Bulls, The Bears and The Pigeons)

A CRASH COURSE IN INVESTING

(The Bulls, The Bears and The Pigeons)

A cartoon comes to mind when I think of stock market advisors. A potential investor is seated at the desk of the stock market guru and says "I would be more inclined to take your advice if I could stop wondering why you still work for a living".

Be aware that it is difficult for a stock broker to be completely objective in giving you stock market advice. He earns his living by your buying and selling securities.

In the world of investing, one comes to a fork in the road. There are guaranteed investments such as government secured certificates of deposit. And there are more riskier investments such as shares traded on a stock market. There is a relationship between the risk of your investment and the yield on your investment. The more risk that you take may lead to a greater reward, or conversely a greater loss. Over a long period of time the stock market has produced larger returns compared to the guaranteed type of investment.

You must decide for yourself what type of investing that you will be more comfortable with, compared to the risk that you choose to take.

There are many asset allocation formulas that brokerage houses suggest. A typical allocation for a mature conservative investor would be:

20% common stocks

25% preferred stocks

25% long term bonds

20% short term bonds

10% money market

Unfortunately, the value of your portfolio may go down as much as 50% the day that you pass away because of estate taxes.

If your investment goals are long term, you can concentrate on growth stocks paying low or no dividends. If you are dependent on receiving income, your investments should lean to more fixed income securities such as bonds or preferred stocks.

COMMON STOCKS

When you purchase a share of common stock you become a part owner in that company. The price of any stock will fluctuate based on several factors:

> world events
>
> interest rates in effect
>
> profits of the company
>
> the current political situation
>
> sectors of the market that are in favor with investors
>
> brokers recommendations
>
> the whims of investors
>
> and any other conceivable reason

There are two major methods of buying stocks. Either you buy an individual stock or you purchase a mutual fund. Either way, it is best to investigate before you invest. Watch the television financial programs, read the financial pages of your newspaper, investigate the history of a company. Some men spend more time choosing a tie than investing in a stock.

A mutual fund is a company which buys various stocks and then sells stock in its own company to the investor at the net asset value, computed at the end of each day.

There are mutual funds that charge the investor a sales charge, called a load, when you make the purchase. Other funds are called no load funds because they have no such sales charge. All funds have an administrative charge to cover their costs and profit. The average administrative charge hovers around one percent. Some funds also charge a "12B1" charge to cover their advertising costs. It is best to avoid buying funds with a load or "12B1" charge. Would you buy a stock today at $ 100 if you were certain that it would go down to $ 94 the same day? In effect, that happens when you buy a load fund that charges a sales charge of 6%.

When buying a mutual fund be aware of the funds total return for one year, three year and ten year period. The total return consists of the dividends and capital gains that you have received plus the increase or decrease in value of the fund for a period of time. Many investors follow the manager of a fund because of his prior success as a manager. Be aware of the type of investments that are made by a mutual fund. Some funds will invest only in one type of market sector, such as technology. Sector funds can be more volatile than more diversified mutual funds. There are large cap, mid size cap and small cap funds. Those labels refer to the total market value of all the outstanding stock of a company.

When buying an individual stock you have the choice of placing your order at the market price, that is the current price that the stock is being sold, or at a limit order which is the price that you choose to pay. Your order will be filled if there is a seller willing to sell his stock to you at the price you have offered.

A so called growth company is one where the expectation is that the company will grow in time. Such companies pay little or no dividends to its stockholders, and generally have higher price earning ratios. If a company earns $ 1.00 per share and its market price is $ 20.00 per share its PE ratio is 20.

A so called value company is one where its market price is considered a fair price based on the fundamentals of the company.

If you were to buy the same stock at different periods of time you would be dollar cost averaging your investment.

One of the ways to measure the volatility of a stock is to know its beta. The average volatility of all stocks is assigned a number one. If a particular stock has a beta of 1 ½ its volatility is one and one half times the average volatility of the market.

There are several indexes that measure the prices of the stock market. The Dow Jones measures 30 large companies selected by the Dow Jones company. The S & P 500 measures 500 stocks selected by the Standard and Poor company. The Russell 2000 measures stocks with smaller market valuations (the total value of a company computed by the number of outstanding shares times the market price). The NASDAC is short for The National Association of Security Dealers which is the body that regulates the activities of security dealers.

PREFERRED STOCKS

As its name suggests, preferred stocks are preferred in one feature. The company that issues preferred stocks must pay dividends on its preferred stocks before paying dividends on its common stock. Also, the preferred stockholders are first to receive liquidations if the company goes out of business. Generally, preferred stocks are not as volatile as common stocks. But they will not generally increase in value as much as common stocks. Its price will be influenced by the quality of the issuing company and the direction of interest rates. The dividend is fixed, unlike the dividends on common stocks. Like any fixed income security, when interest rates increase the price of a preferred stock will decrease. When interest rates decrease, the price of a preferred stock will increase. Most companies issue preferred stock at an initial offering price $25.00 per share. If you buy the stock at its initial offering price (IPO) you will not pay any commission on the purchase.

BONDS

A bond issued by a company is similar to its I O U. It represents the debt of the company. On the other hand, common stock represents the equity of the company. The market price of a bond is influenced by the quality of the issuing company and the direction of interest rates. Just as with preferred stocks, when interest rates increase, the market price of a bond will decrease. When interest rates decrease, the price of a bond will increase. When you buy a bond, your broker will quote you its price and yield. If you buy it at par (the original issuing price), the stated dividend and yield will be the same. If you buy it at a discount (less than its original issuing price), your yield will be higher than the stated dividend. Conversely, if you buy it at a premium (higher than its original issuing price), your yield will be lower than the stated dividend. Most bonds have a call feature which allows the company to call the bond, that is to cancel the bond and pay you a preagreed price to cancel the bond. The call date is a specific date. For example a call date may be five years from the issue date of the bond. Therefore it is important for you to know the yield on the bond to its call date should the bond be called. It is also important to know the current yield which will be based on the stated dividend in relation to the price you paid for the bond. Also, be aware of the yield to the maturity of the bond, which is based on the stated dividend in relation to the price you paid for the bond, considering the number of years to maturity.

The longer the maturity of a bond the higher is the risk of price fluctuation. For example, if there is a 1% increase in the prime rate after you buy a bond, there will be a 10% drop in the market price of a bond with a 20 year maturity.

Consider the rating of a bond. Triple A (AAA) is the best rating. Double A (AA) is next. Then comes single A, BBB, BB, B, and C. A rating of less than BBB is considered less than investment grade and should be avoided if you are conservative. So call junk bonds are those with speculative ratings.

As mentioned before, the market price of bonds will fluctuate with the prime rate. The prime rate is the rate banks will charge their best credit worthy customers.

A technique to average the yields on bonds is to ladder your purchases. That is to buy bonds with different maturity dates. The different maturity dates will generally offer different yields.

TAX FREE MUNICIPAL BONDS

The obvious advantage of owning a "muni", a tax free municipal bond, is that you pay no income tax on the interest that you receive. If you are in the 28% income tax bracket, receiving a 6% yield on a muni is equivalent to receiving 8.33% on a taxable security. So, always consider the equivalent yield when buying a muni.

Muni's are always sold to you by a broker from his inventory of the ones that his firm owns. There is no commission charged when you buy. The broker marks up the price he paid and charges you a higher price. The only way you can determine if you are being charged a good price is to compare the price of the same bond, with the same interest rate and maturity date, with another broker.

Again, you should be aware of the rating of a bond, the current yield as well as the yield to call and yield to maturity.

Municipal bonds can be bought individually or through a municipal bond mutual fund.

ZERO COUPON BONDS

This is a bond which pays no current rate of interest. It is sold to you at a lower price and is redeemed, when it is due, at a higher price.

The yield of such an investment is generally slightly higher than that of a comparable bond which pays interest currently. However you receive no income during the term of the bond. The resale value of a zero coupon bond may also be less than of a bond which pays interest currently.

DEFERRED ANNUITIES

These are sold through insurance companies. They can have a fixed rate of return or a variable rate determined by the investments in the various mutual funds that you choose that are offered by the insurance company. Until you withdraw money from the deferred annuity, you pay no tax on the income earned. When you do withdraw, those sums are considered ordinary taxable income until the value of the annuity equals your original investment. You do not get the advantage received by paying reduced long term capital gains taxes on investments held over one year that you own outside of the annuity.

Some annuities will charge you a surrender charge if you make withdrawals in excess of a stated amount within a certain period of time. Since there is some life insurance coverage there is a life insurance annual charge built into the annuity contract.

INDEX FUNDS

Index funds reflect the stocks included in a particular combination of stocks. For example, a Dow Jones index fund will increase or decrease in price in relationship to the Dow Jones industrial average of 30 stocks. The QQQ, which is another index fund, reflects the prices of the stocks included in the Nasdac 100 combination of stocks.

CLOSED END FUNDS - UNIT INVESTMENT TRUSTS

This is a mutual fund which stops selling to the public after its initial public offering. As contrasted to the usual mutual fund which continuously keeps selling shares. The C E F sells it I P O to the public and then stops offering shares from that point on. While it is in existence, the fund will sell securities in its portfolio and buy other securities.

A feature of the C E F is that the market price after the I P O generally goes down. It is not unusual for a C E F to sell at discounts of 10 - 20 % below its net asset value.

STOCK BROKERS

It is best to leave your broker hold your securities. Check to determine how much insurance is provided by your broker. Allowing your broker to hold your securities is much safer than if you have physical possession. It is convenient for your broker to collect all dividends and credit your account or send you a check for the income received. The broker keeps track of stock splits. A split occurs, as an example, when a company decides to issue you an additional share of stock that you own. You will find it helpful to receive a monthly statement showing the market value of all securities that you own and the balance of your money market account that you may have with the broker. At the end of the year you will receive one Form 1099 from the broker indicating all interest and dividends received for the year, as well as a summary of all securities that you sold during the year. Most brokers provide you with a checking account for your money market funds, and will credit you with higher interest than most banks do on money market accounts. A broker can be helpful in guiding you to your investment decisions. Keep in mind that it is your money and your responsibility to make your investment decisions. Use

lots of common sense.

KEEP IN MIND WHEN INVESTING

Know your time frame you intend to hold a stock

Keep sales commissions low

Don't put all your eggs in one basket. Allocate your assets among

various types of investments

Don't diversify too much or too little

Understand what you are buying

Educate yourself by reading the financial news, magazines, and

watching financial television programs

Be aware of the direction of interest rates

Don't buy a stock and then forget about it

Dollar cost averaging reduces risk

Avoid risk by buying established successful companies

Investigate before you invest

Consider using a financial advisor if you do not have the time or inclination to monitor your investments

Remember that it is your money and your responsibility

Use common sense

RULE OF 72

The expression "double your money" is often used. It may be helpful to be aware of a simple formula to accomplish "doubling your money". Any two numbers which multiplied by each other equals 72 will accomplish this phenomenon.

For example:

At a 6% rate of return, it will take 12 years to double your original investment. (6 x 12 = 72)

At a 9% rate of return, it will take 8 years to double your original investment. (9 x 8 = 72)

At a 10% rate of return, it will take 7.2 years to double your original investment. (10 x 7.2 = 72)

THE BEST INVESTMENT

The best investment is not necessarily the one with the greatest return. It is one where you can sleep at night.

It was Will Rogers who said "I am less worried about the return on my investment and more worried about the return of my investment."

HOW LONG WILL YOUR MONEY LAST?

HOW LONG WILL YOUR MONEY LAST?

Many of us are concerned that we will outlive our money and be left penniless. It is important to be aware of the variables and the arithmetic involved in the computation of how long will your money last.

For example:

your assets total	$ 500,000	$ 500,000
you earn, per year	6%	10%
you withdraw, the first year	10%	10%
you withdraw the second year	10.4%	10.4%
you withdraw the third year	10.82%	10.82%
you continue to increase your withdrawals by an assumed inflation rate of 4%		
your money will become zero in	11 years	14 years

It becomes obvious that you have to plan the relationship between the rate of income that you earn in relationship to the withdrawals of the principal that you make.

HOW TO RECONCILE YOUR CHECK BOOK

BALANCE WITH YOUR BANK STATEMENT

HOW TO RECONCILE YOUR CHECK BOOK

BALANCE WITH YOUR BANK STATEMENT

Some people ask "How can my account be overdrawn if I still have blank checks in my check book?"

If you can add one and one to equal two you can reconcile your check book to your bank statement. If you can do simple arithmetic you are capable of reconciling your bank statement.

The basic theory of creating a check book balance is to start with a correct balance in your check book, add deposits made and subtract checks written.

Example

balance at beginning	$ 4,010.22
add: deposit made	356.87
total	$ 4,367.09
less: check written	443.46

balance $ 3,923.63

If your check book stub is designed to keep track of your balance one entry at a time, the above example would coincide with your entries in your check book.

Some checkbook stubs are designed to allow you to enter three checks on a page. If so, compute your check book balance on the blank side of your check book stub, using the same method as shown above.

Now comes the day of reckoning - your bank statement comes in the mail. Your bank shows a different balance than your check book balance. Of course the bank has a different balance. The date of your bank statement is different than your current check book balance. Also, there may be entries on your bank statement not yet entered in your check book, such as interest credited to your account or bank charges deducted from your account.

The first thing to do is to trace the checks returned by the bank to your check book stub. In this way you will know which checks have not been returned by the bank (called outstanding checks). Then compare the deposits entered in your check book with the deposits credited by the bank.

Your check book balance will agree with the bank statement balance after taking into consideration various items, which are as follows:

bank charges that the bank has charged you

interest credited to your account by the bank

outstanding checks (checks written by you but not yet returned by the bank)

outstanding deposits (deposits that you have made but not credited by the bank)

Example:

MY CHECKBOOK BALANCE		$ 6,003.67
ADD: OUTSTANDING CHECKS		567.44
INTEREST CREDITED		5.10
TOTAL		$ 6,576.21
LESS: BANK CHARGES	$ 12.50	

OUTSTANDING DEPOSI   900.00

TOTAL $ 912.50

THIS SHOULD BE THE BANK BALANCE $ 5,663.71

If, at this point, you do not reconcile your check book balance with the bank statement balance, do the following:

1. look at the bank statement to see any miscellaneous charges or credits

2. check the arithmetic of your reconciliation

3. check the arithmetic of your check book

4. verify the outstanding checks

5. verify the outstanding deposit

After you do reconcile, you will feel great!

HOW TO RECONCILE YOUR STOCK BROKER

OR MUTUAL FUND STATEMENT

HOW TO RECONCILE YOUR STOCK BROKER OR

MUTUAL FUND STATEMENT

There are two important items to verify on your monthly statement, after verifying the current months purchases and sales of stock.

1. Your money market or cash balance
2. Your stocks being held by the broker.

YOUR MONEY MARKET OR CASH BALANCE

This balance should be reconciled in the same manner as you reconcile your check book with your bank statement. See the chapter "How to reconcile your check book with your bank statement". If your broker provides you with a check book stub that is convenient to use in computing your balance, do use it to compute your balance. If it is not a convenient stub to use, create a page similar to the following:

81

	IN	OUT	BALANCE
<u>Beginning balance</u>			$ 2010.00
<u>add:</u>			
dividends received			
ATT	$ 100.00		2,110.00
Xyz co.	50.00		2,160.00
money market	20.00		2,180.00
<u>less:</u>			
stocks bought			
ABC Co.		$ 1,081.50	
Balance			$ 1,098.50

YOUR STOCKS BEING HELD BY YOUR BROKER

Compare your position (the stocks, bonds, mutual funds, preferred stocks, etc. that you own) at the end of this month with your positions at the end of last month, taking into consideration any stocks, bonds, etc. that you bought or sold during the month.

If you are unsure of any items which appear on your statement, ask your broker about them.

THE DETAILS OF YOUR BROKERAGE STATEMENT

No two brokerage houses use the same computer program to generate its statements sent to customers. But they all resemble each other and are basically similar in content. Let us go through a typical brokerage statement sent to you at the end of each month.

ACCOUNT VALUATION

Total market value at the end of last month and at the end of this month, broken down as follows:

Cash and cash equivalents (money market)

Equities (individual stocks)

Mutual Funds

Municipal Bonds (bonds with nontaxable income)

Total assets

Compare the total assets at the end of this month with the total assets at the end of last month, adjusted for any new funds put into your account, or funds withdrawn, to quickly see how your investments have increased or decreased in market value during the month.

ASSET ALLOCATION

This tells you what percentages of your total assets are invested in cash, equities, mutual funds of municipal bonds, etc. This is a convenient chart in which you can see the categories of your investments.

REGULAR ACCOUNT ACTIVITY

The entries in this section of your brokerage account itemizes all increases or decreases in your account caused by the following events:

dividends received

funds transferred from other accounts

sales of stock you sold

purchases you made of securities

money market checks you wrote

other items charged or credited

EQUITIES

This section shows you details of the securities that you own, such as:

name of security

stock symbol of the security

Cusip number - the number assigned to each security

quantity of shares you own

market price at the date of the statement

total market value - the number of shares times the market price of each share

MUTUAL FUNDS

Contains the same details as described in the Equities section.

HOW LONG SHOULD FINANCIAL RECORDS

BE KEPT?

HOW LONG SHOULD FINANCIAL RECORDS BE KEPT?

Keep indefinitely, or until three years after its sale, documents relating to the following:

purchase of your home

purchase of stocks, bonds and other investments

title to your home

purchase deed

mortgage papers

receipts for home improvements

receipts for items covered by insurance

copies of all tax returns for three years after filing

broker confirmations for purchases and sales of stocks

You can be audited by Internal Revenue Service within a three year period after filing your return. There is no statute of limitations if fraud is suspected. If audited you will be asked to provide supporting documents to prove deductible expenses taken on your return and to establish your cost basis of securities or other investments sold.

There is a seven year statute of limitations regarding commercial debts. It is most unusual for a creditor to wait that long to collect an amount due to him.

Bank statements, credit card and brokerage statements can be discarded after the time for auditing your tax return is past.

INCOME TAXES

INCOME TAXES

Chances are that you will go to an accountant to prepare your personal income tax.

What information will your accountant need?

> Your prior years income tax returns
>
> All wage statements (W 2)
>
> Distributions received from pension plans
>
> Income and expenses of a business you own
>
> Real estate rental income and expenses
>
> Payments made re: estimated taxes

> All forms 1099 that you receive (indicating interest and dividends received)
>
> All K-1 forms
>
> > You receive those for all partnership or subchapter S corporation income. A subchapter S corporation is

one that has elected to pay no income taxes and has its shareholders pay their personal income taxes on the income earned by the corporation based on their percentage of stock owned.

All annual brokerage statements

The brokers statement will provide information regarding interest and dividends earned and sales of securities. Some brokers will compute the gain or loss on each sale.

All other items of income received

Itemized Deductions That You Can Claim To Reduce Your Taxes

Medical and dental expenses

State and local income taxes

Real estate taxes

Personal Property taxes

Interest and points paid on mortgages

Interest paid on investments

Gifts paid to charities

Casualty and theft losses

Expenses in connection with your job

Tax preparation fees

Investment expenses

How Can You Reduce Your Income Tax?

Invest in tax free municipal bonds or tax free municipal bond funds. However, you must compare the income you receive from a tax free bond with the after tax income you receive from a taxable investment. For example, compare a yield of 5% earned on a muni bond with a 8% earned on a preferred stock.

Do the arithmetic:

8% x 28% (assuming that you are in that tax bracket, including state taxes) = 5.76% net income after taxes

5.76% after taxes on an investment of 8% before taxes is better than 5% earned on a tax free investment.

But there are other factors to consider before making a decision. Compare the rating of one security to the other. Compare the ability to sell one security to the other. Both securities change in value each day based on market conditions. Selling a preferred stock is different than selling a muni bond. The price of the preferred stock is quoted in the newspaper daily. When you sell you will receive the current price less commission paid to the broker. There is no readily available price quote for your individual muni bond. You can only get a price by calling your broker to find out what his firm is willing to pay you for your bond. Bonds are generally sold to you by the broker from his inventory of bonds that he owns. It is not unusual for a broker to add 2% to his cost when selling you a bond, or deduct 2% from the market price when buying a bond from you. Brokers charge no commissions for buying or selling muni bonds because they make their money on the "mark up".

Have Long Term Gains In The Market - Not Short Term

Under present law you pay income tax on capital gains based on whether you have held the stock for less or more than twelve months. Sales of stock held over twelve months are taxed at a reduced but no more than 20% tax. If you own a stock for less than twelve months and are considering selling it, you should make a judgment decision whether to hold the stock for the twelve month period before selling in order to be taxed at the 20% level, taking into consideration the possible change in market value when you sell.

Contribute To A Tax Deferred I R A, Pension Plan or 401 K Plan

This is an excellent way to reduce current income taxes and continue to earn tax deferred income on these contributions as long as the money remains in such a tax deferred account.

For those people who are conducting a business, a pension plan has such benefits. You can create a simple profit sharing and/or a money purchase plan. The usual way to maximize benefits is to have a 10%

money purchase plan plus a profit sharing plan of up to 15% of your salary from the corporation or net profit from self employment. The 10% must be contributed each year to the plan. The profit sharing plan is flexible. Each year you determine whether or not to make a contribution in any amount up to 15% of your salary taken. There is a maximum amount which can be contributed to such plans. Generally, all employees must be included in the plans. Most brokerage houses will supply you with a prototype plan, preapproved by Internal Revenue Service, without charge.

Individuals who are employees will get tax savings by participating in a company sponsored plan, a 401 K plan, especially in one where the company contributes its share to the employees contribution. If your company does not have a 401 K plan, you can contribute up to $ 3,000.00 per year to your own I. R. A. plan, or if married, up to $ 6000.00, for the years 2002, 2003, 2004, with higher amounts allowed in later years.

BEFORE YOU HIRE AN ACCOUNTANT OR

ATTORNEY

BEFORE YOU HIRE AN ACCOUNTANT OR ATTORNEY

Interview him

ask regarding fee for initial interview

determine if you feel comfortable with him

does he listen to you?

ask about his education or special training

does he have sufficient experience?

discuss alternatives to his suggestions

determine the approximate fee that you will be charged for his services

THE LANGUAGE OF ESTATE PLANNING

THE LANGUAGE OF ESTATE PLANNING

DURABLE POWER OF ATTORNEY

> empowers the person holding the power of attorney to act on your behalf - does not cease in case of your disability - ceases at your death

EXECUTOR, ADMINSTRATOR OR PERSONAL REPRESENTATIVE

> these are interchangeable terms, depending on the state you live in - this is the person who will carry out the provisions of your Last Will

GUARDIAN

> the individual designated to handle your affairs in the event that you are deemed incapable

HEALTH CARE POWER OF ATTORNEY

> the individual designated to make medical decisions for you in the event that you are incapable

INTESTACY

in the event you die leaving no Will or Revocable Living Trust, you are intestate - your assets will be distributed according to state law

LIVING WILL

your declaration, in writing, that you do not wish to be resuscitated in the event you are brain dead

LAST WILL

your Will recites your wishes regarding the distribution of whatever you own after your death

POWER OF ATTORNEY

empowers the person holding the power of attorney to act on your behalf - ceases at your death or disability

PROBATE

the court process required to transfer property held in your name
even though its disposition is provided in your Will - probate can
be avoided for assets held in a Revocable Living Trust

PERSONAL RESIDENCE TRUST

ownership of your personal residence is placed into such a Trust
which provides for the following:

You have the right to live in the residence for a specific
number of years of your choice with no payment to the Trust. You
continue to pay taxes, maintenance, mortgage payments, etc.

At the end of that term the residence can be owned by the
person that you designate in the Trust.

You will enter into a lease with that person to continue to live
in the residence and pay a rent based upon the fair market value.

PRENUPTIAL AGREEMENT

a written agreement made between two people prior to their marriage outlining their rights in the event of death or divorce

POUR OVER WILL

a Will made in conjunction with a Revocable Living Trust providing for the disposition of assets not held by the Revocable Living Trust

REVOCABLE LIVING TRUST

a set of papers, prepared by an attorney, which describes your wishes regarding the assets held by the Trust while you are alive and also after your death

TRUSTS

a separate legal entity created to hold assets

the grantor -   the person making the trust and

transferring assets to the trust

the beneficiary -   the person for whom the trust was created and who will receive its income or principal

the trustee -   the person holding legal title to the trust assets and is responsible for its investments and distributions

UNIFIED TAX CREDIT OR LIFETIME EXEMPTION

the amount exempt from estate taxes - $ 1,000,000.00 for the years 2002 and 2003, increasing in various amounts until it reaches $ 3,500,000.00 in the year 2009.

UNLIMITED MARITAL DEDUCTION

transfers between spouses are nontaxable during their lifetime or after death

ABOUT THE AUTHOR

Harry Mautner is a Certified Public Accountant practicing in New York and Florida, specializing in estate planning and taxes. He has lectured extensively on these subjects on television, in universities and has conducted seminars on cruise ships. He was a major stockholder and officer of publicly held corporations. He has been the executor or personal representative of several estates in New York and Florida.

He lives with his wife in Hollywood, Florida. His immediate family includes their two sons, daughter in law and two grandchildren.

www.ingramcontent.com/pod-product-compliance
Lightning Source LLC
Chambersburg PA
CBHW021544290526
45785CB00004BA/1512